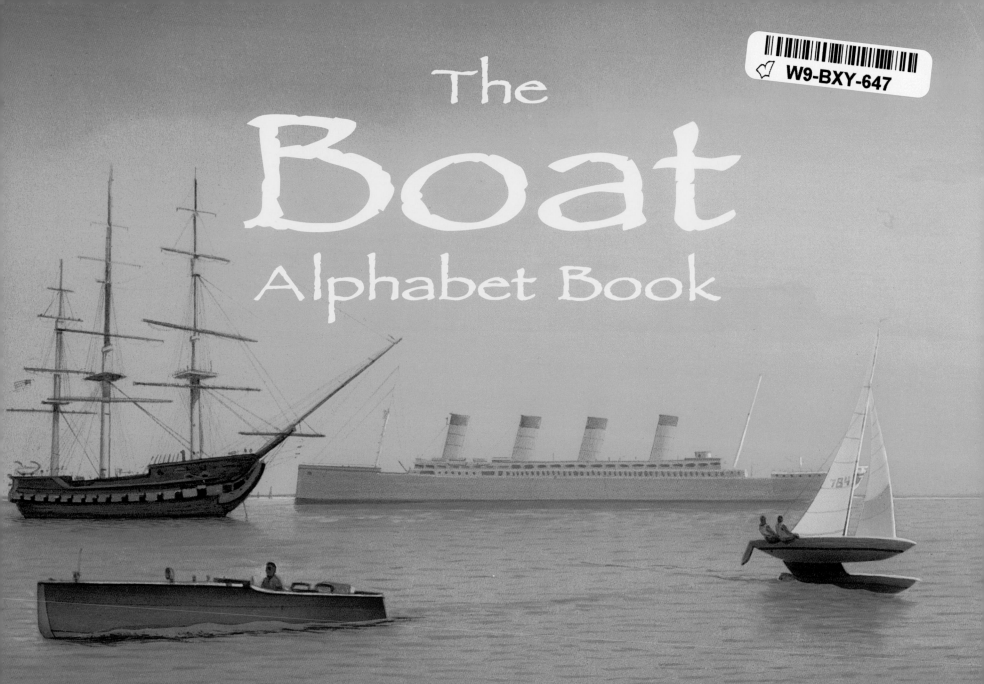

The Boat
Alphabet Book

JERRY PALLOTTA

ILLUSTRATED BY DAVID BIEDRZYCKI

Charlesbridge

In memory of A. J. McEachern:
nephew, mosser, lobsterer, water-skier, sailor, clammer, surfer, nice kid,
and the best striped-bass fisherman.
—Jerry Pallotta
Peggotty Beach, 8/4/97

For Wally and Nell.

Special thanks to Sue and Bruce Tobiasson,
Jane Archer, Carolyn O'Leary, and of course, Jerry.
—David Biedrzycki
42°11'15" N   71°18'25" W

2003 First paperback edition
Text copyright © 1998 by Jerry Pallotta
Illustrations copyright © 1998 by David Biedrzycki
All rights reserved, including the right of reproduction in
whole or in part in any form. Charlesbridge and colophon
are registered trademarks of Charlesbridge Publishing, Inc.

Published by Charlesbridge
85 Main Street, Watertown, MA 02472
(617) 926-0329
www.charlesbridge.com

Printed and bound April 2010 by Sung In Printing
in Gunpo-Si, Kyonggi-Do, Korea
(hc) 10 9 8 7 6 5 4 3
(sc) 10 9 8 7 6

Illustrations done in acrylic on Strathmore illustration board

Library of Congress Cataloging-in-Publication Data
Pallotta, Jerry.
    The boat alphabet book/by Jerry Pallotta; illustrated
by David Biedrzycki.
        p.   cm.
    Summary: An alphabet book presenting unusual
facts about a variety of boats and ships from aircraft
carriers to zodiacs.
    ISBN-13: 978-0-88106-910-5; ISBN-10: 0-88106-910-8 (reinforced for library use)
    ISBN-13: 978-0-88106-911-2; ISBN-10: 0-88106-911-6 (softcover)
1. Boats and boating—Miscellanea—Juvenile literature.
[1. Boats and boating. 2. Alphabet.] I. Biedrzycki, David,
ill. II. Title.
VM150.P3   1998
623.8'2—dc21
[E]   97-39442

Did you ever wonder why the first boat was built? Was it to cross a lake, to travel down a river, to explore, or just to have fun? And what did the first boat look like? Maybe it was a log or a carved-out tree. Whatever it was, those first sailors probably never imagined . . .

. . . an Aircraft Carrier.

Aa

A is for Aircraft Carrier. This military ship is a floating airport. An Aircraft Carrier can carry more than one hundred aircraft: fighter jets, planes, and helicopters. It is also a floating city! About 6,000 people work and live on the largest Aircraft Carriers. On board, you will find a church, movie theater, library, hospital, dental office, post office, and even a barbershop.

Each day, the barbers give over 250 haircuts, the cooks bake 800 loaves of bread, the crew drinks 13,000 cans of soda, and the kitchen staff sometimes serves up to 10,000 hamburgers! There are almost 2,000 telephones on board and 30,000 lights. What would you do if the captain said, "It's your turn to shut off all the lights"?

Bb

B is for Barkentine. There are many different kinds of tall ships. Some of these are brigs, barks, brigantines, frigates, schooners, and clippers. This tall ship is a Barkentine. It has square sails on its foremast and staysails on its mainmast, mizzenmast, and jiggermast.

Cc

C is for Canoe. Of all the boats in this book, the Canoe is probably the most popular. Canoes are light and easy to launch. They are perfect for boating on lakes and small rivers. Just paddle out, and the Canoe will bring you closer to nature.

Dd

D is for Dory. Dories are flat-bottomed wooden workboats. Many years ago, they were used for a type of commercial fishing called longlining. Today, Dories are used for clamming, lobstering, harvesting seaweed, and going for a nice, relaxing row.

E is for Electric Boat. Some people call a nuclear-powered submarine an Electric Boat. Is it really a boat? Yes and no. A submarine can float on the surface like a boat but can also travel underwater. Electric Boats can circumnavigate the earth without ever surfacing.

Ee

Ff

F is for Ferry. A Ferry is a boat that carries passengers or cars from one dock to another. Older Ferries have steel hulls. Newer aluminum Ferries are faster and give smoother rides.

The hull is the outer shell of the boat. The bow is the front of the boat, and the stern is the rear.

BAY STATE CRUISES

M/V VINEYARD SPRAY

Gg

G is for Gondola. Gondolas are water taxis. The city of Venice, Italy, is famous for Gondola travel because its roads are canals. Sometimes the gondoliers sing to their passengers. Watch out! Things could get romantic.

Hh

H is for Hydrofoil. When docked, it looks like any other boat. When traveling at high speeds, the Hydrofoil lifts up and skims the surface like a water-skier. With less friction from the water, the boat can zoom along faster.

I is for Icebreaker. When winter comes and the waterways freeze, most boats and ships cannot get through. The Icebreaker can! This vessel, with its extra-thick hull, can smash through the ice and make a passageway for itself and other boats that might follow.

I i

Jj

J is for Junk. This Chinese ship with the high poop deck is called a Junk. Even when it is brand new, it is still called a Junk. Legend has it that some people were born on Junks and spent their entire lives on board without ever setting foot on land.

Kk

K is for Kayak. The earliest
Kayaks were made from walrus or
seal skin that was stretched over
bone or wooden frames. Today,
Kayaks are popular both for
pleasure and for sport and are
made of synthetic "skins" such as
rubber, plastic, and fiberglass.

Ll

L is for Lightship. This ship is a floating, movable lighthouse. Lightships can be anchored in locations where it might not be possible to build a lighthouse. Lightships and lighthouses warn sailors of dangerous waters so that they can navigate around them.

SIOUX FALLS

On this page, slow down and be careful.
There are mines in the water.

M is for Minesweeper. Mines are
floating bombs. A Minesweeper is
used to remove or destroy them.
Many mines are detonated by
the magnetism of steel.
Minesweepers are made
of wood. They don't
even have steel nails.

Mm

Nn

N is for Nao. In the journals that Christopher Columbus kept during his first voyage to North America, he referred to his ship, the *Santa Maria*, as a Nao. What was a Nao? Was it a specific type of sailing ship used for trade, or was "nao" simply an old Spanish word meaning "ship"? No one knows for sure.

O is for Ocean Liner. It's party time! Ocean Liners are floating resort hotels made especially for people on vacation. These ships cruise all over the world. During a fourteen-day trip, an Ocean Liner might anchor at many different islands and cities. If you like ships, music, dancing, and eating, then an Ocean Liner is for you.

Oo

P is for Pedalboat. If you can pedal a bicycle, you can get this boat moving. The harder you pedal, the faster it goes. This boat is human powered.

If you want to call it a pontoon boat or a paddleboat, that's OK, too.

Pp

Q is for Quffa. This is a basket boat. Quffas are usually found on the Tigris and Euphrates Rivers. Some are so large that twenty people can fit inside one without sinking. Quffa can also be spelled guffa, gufa, gufah, or khuffa.

Qq

R is for Reed Boat. Reeds are a type of fat, hollow grass. After years of watching reeds float by, someone probably had the brilliant idea of tying hundreds of them together to make a boat. The idea worked. A Reed Boat could have been the first boat ever built.

Rr

Ss

S is for Steamboat. Some of the first boat engines were steam powered. A Steamboat engine works like this: Hot coals boil water. The water becomes steam. The steam expands, and the pressure drives pistons up and down. The moving pistons turn a giant paddle wheel, and the boat is propelled through the water. Today, Steamboats are outdated but are sometimes used as tourist attractions and casinos.

T t

T is for Tanker. Tankers are ships that carry liquids. Most tankers carry oil products such as crude oil, diesel fuel, home heating oil, kerosene, grease, and gasoline. Let's hope this ship is double hulled so that if it runs aground, nothing will spill out. What else could a tanker be carrying? Maybe chocolate milk!

Uu

Remember the K page? A kayak is a closed boat that fits snugly around a person's waist. Traditionally, it was a one-man hunting boat.

Here is a traditional "woman's boat."

U is for Umiak. The Umiak is an open boat that is designed for more than one person. It can hold a mother, her children, dogs, and supplies. Umiak is pronounced "OO-mee-ack."

V v

V is for Viking Ship. It is easy to admire the wooden ships that were built by the adventurous Scandinavian pirates, the Vikings. These fast, seaworthy ships were strong enough to cross oceans, yet light enough to sail up shallow rivers.

The cleverly designed Viking Ships were built with simple iron tools. A Viking shipbuilder would use an auger, a chisel, an adze, a hammer, lots of nails, and most importantly, an ax.

W w

W is for Windjammer. Windjammer is a term for any large sailing vessel, like this schooner. Windjammer is also an old slang word for people who prefer boats with sails over boats with engines. Let's go windjamming!

Xx

X is for Xebec. A Xebec is a three-masted ship that is rigged with lateen sails. It is very similar to another boat, a dhow. This Xebec had three sails, but one of them must have been ripped by rough, stormy weather.

Y is for Yacht. When you become rich and famous, you can own a luxurious yacht. Then you can go anywhere you want. Let's sail to Aruba, Bimini, Cuba, Dominica, Easter Island, Fiji, Grenada, Haiti, Isla Mujeres, Jamaica, Kodiak, Long Island, Montserrat, Nantucket, Oahu, Pitcairn Island, Qeshm, Rat Island, Seychelles, Tahiti, Ulithi, Virgin Gorda, Weddell Island, Xizhong, Yap, and Zanzibar.

Yy

Z is for Zodiac.
A Zodiac is an inflatable boat.
The company that built zeppelins
decided to use the same technology to
build boats. At first glance, a Zodiac looks like
a giant toy you would find in a swimming pool.
However, Zodiacs are quite seaworthy, and zillions
of Zodiacs are now used all over the world.

Z z

Here is a bell buoy, a navigational aid. Usually a bell buoy marks the entrance to a harbor. But right now, this bell buoy marks the end of the book!